Bon Jovi
live!

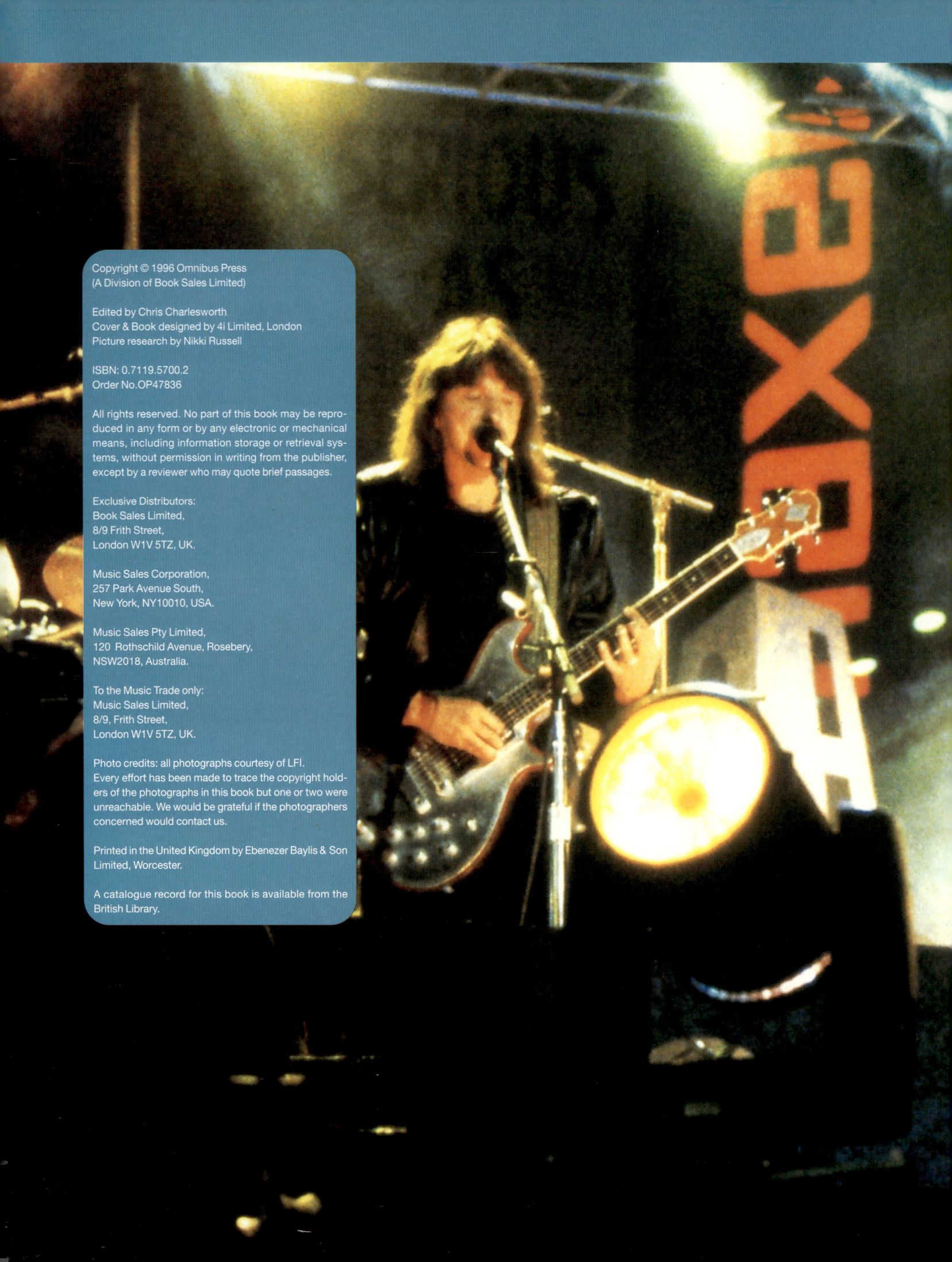

Copyright © 1996 Omnibus Press
(A Division of Book Sales Limited)

Edited by Chris Charlesworth.
Cover & Book designed by 4i Limited, London
Picture research by Nikki Russell

ISBN: 0.7119.5700.2
Order No.OP47836

All rights reserved. No part of this book may be reproduced in any form or by any electronic or mechanical means, including information storage or retrieval systems, without permission in writing from the publisher, except by a reviewer who may quote brief passages.

Exclusive Distributors:
Book Sales Limited,
8/9 Frith Street,
London W1V 5TZ, UK.

Music Sales Corporation,
257 Park Avenue South,
New York, NY10010, USA.

Music Sales Pty Limited,
120 Rothschild Avenue, Rosebery,
NSW2018, Australia.

To the Music Trade only:
Music Sales Limited,
8/9, Frith Street,
London W1V 5TZ, UK.

Photo credits: all photographs courtesy of LFI.
Every effort has been made to trace the copyright holders of the photographs in this book but one or two were unreachable. We would be grateful if the photographers concerned would contact us.

Printed in the United Kingdom by Ebenezer Baylis & Son Limited, Worcester.

A catalogue record for this book is available from the British Library.

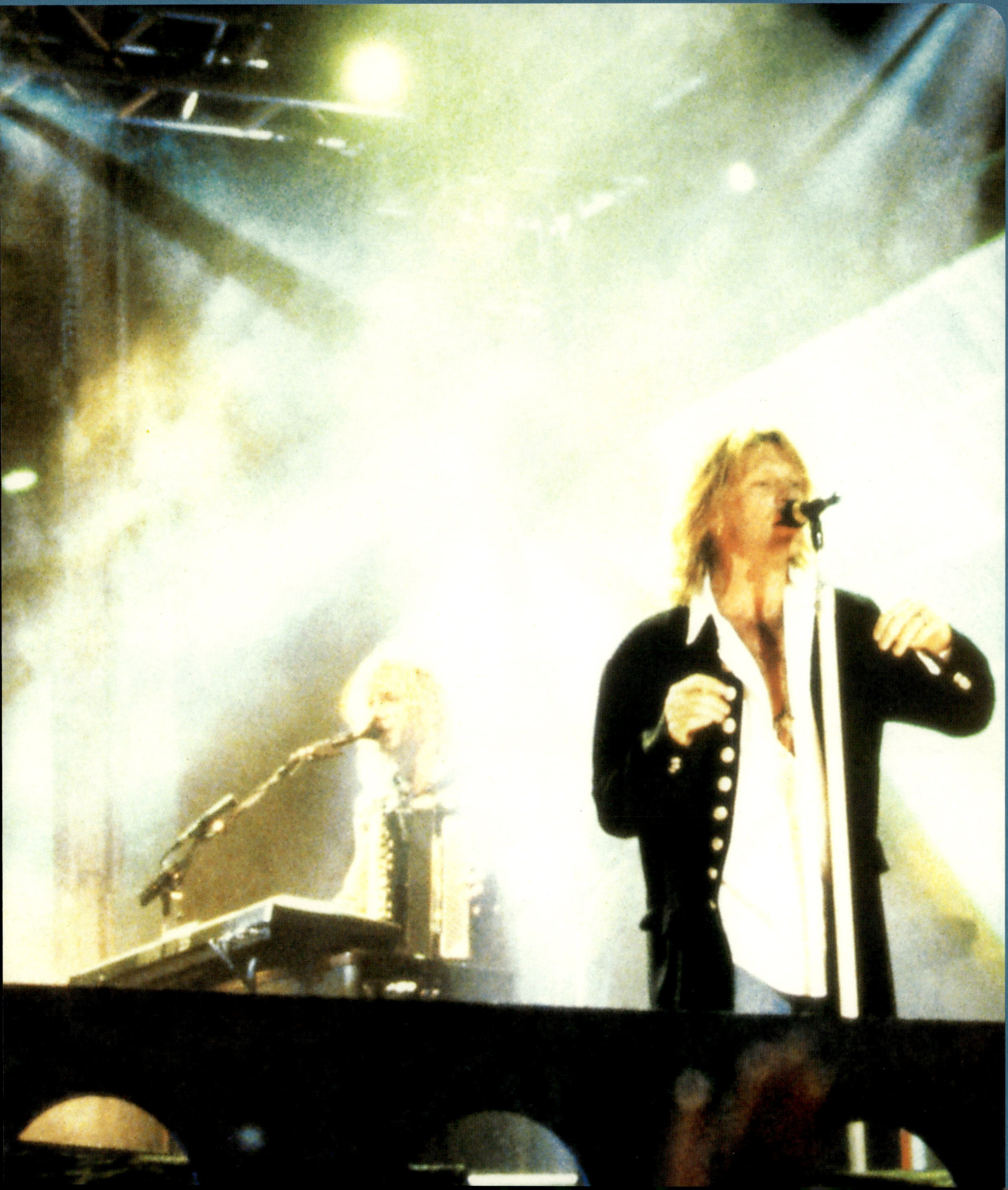

BY NOW we are all familiar with the name and the face: Jon Bon Jovi. Better looking than the best-looking boy at school. Better still, fronting one of the biggest and best rock and roll bands ever. Songs like 'You Give Love A Bad Name', 'Livin' On A Prayer' or 'Always' aren't just great Bon Jovi numbers, they're, classic, timeless rock songs – part of the sweep of the great American dream, siphoned through the reality of life in the raw.

The story of Bon Jovi and the band he gave his name to is as romantic as any of their best songs, too. The classic rags-to-riches rock and roll yarn of one boy and his unbridled desire and determination to get to the top – the story of Bon Jovi would have made for a great Hollywood movie, except who'd believe it?

Jon Bon Jovi superstar was in fact born plain John Bongiovi Jnr. on March 2, 1962, in New Jersey. He got given his first guitar as a Christmas present when he was seven, and soon displayed a keen interest in making music. "While the rest of the kids were out playing baseball or whatever, I was in my room learning how to stand in front of a mirror with a guitar in my hands," he once recalled. His first local band were called Starz, formed at High School. After one gig they became Raze, who played their first (and last) ever show of any note at a High School talent contest – they finished last.

At this stage, Jon flirted briefly with becoming an actor, playing a local theatre version of the hit musical *Mame* and auditioning for the star-role in the movie *Footloose* which was originally about a struggling rock singer. But it was the rock scene that soon recaptured the young Bongiovi's imagination.

After Raze's inevitable demise, he formed a rambling R&B band called Atlantic City Expressway (ACE), which became a popular fixture on the local New Jersey club scene.

ACE also saw John hook up for the first time with a talented young keyboards player called David Rashbaum. Despite the patronage of Jersey shoreline legends such as Bruce Springsteen and Southside Johnny, who were both known for getting up and doing a number or two with the band, ACE never really progressed. When they, too, eventually disintegrated, John changed musical tack completely and became the frontman with a far more new wave-oriented local Jersey outfit called The Rest. Although there was label interest from Columbia, with both Southside Johnny and, notably, Billy Squier – a huge star in the US at the time – producing demos for the band, The Rest never quite managed to break out of the local scene and eventually frustration led to acrimony and the band broke up.

With The Rest, er, put to rest, John seriously began to wonder if he was ever going to get the break he needed. In September, 1980, he took up an offer of a low-paid job at the celebrated Power Station Studios in New York which were owned by his second cousin Tony Bongiovi. At the time the studio was being used by people like Mick Jagger and David Bowie, and John took every opportunity to watch and learn. "I started out as a gofer," he says. "You know, go for this, go for that – sandwiches, coffee, cigarettes, whatever. Sweeping up. I tell ya, though, I learned a lot pushing that broom. There was all kinds of people working there and I just studied everything."

While he was acting as the local dogs body, he was also learning from the pros and putting it into his own demos. Whenever there was spare time in the studios (usually during 'dead time', early hours before dawn when the rest of the world is sleeping), John was in the studio working away at his own imaginary album. By Christmas 1982, a tape labelled 'Johnny B' featuring, among other songs, a catchy little number called 'Runaway', began to circulate in New York. Major labels began sniffing, and a showcase gig was set up for John and his occasional backing band of friends and fellow gofers, now called The Wild Ones and featuring among others Rashbaum and future Skid Row guitarist Dave 'Snake' Sabo.

The venue was the Ritz, in New York, and the occasion was a support slot to his old pals and mentors, Southside Johnny & The Asbury Dukes. It was supposed to have been the best thing he'd ever done, the big breakthrough. Instead, it proved a disaster, nearly finishing off his chances of stardom before he'd even got a record out.

Realising that his novelty value in New York was wearing intolerably thin and still determined "to prove them all wrong – that's always been a major motivation", John decided to up sticks and move to Los Angeles with Rashbaum and batter down the doors of the music business moguls on the west coast. At one point they set up stall in a room in a motel and just invited record company A&R people to just come by and hear them sing. They spent their days hawking tapes around to anyone that would give them the time of day – agents, club owners, record label employees. The result was a few gig offers and a couple of encouraging 'maybes'.

"It was clear that whatever coast you worked from, the problems were the same," says John. "Getting people to believe in it. In you." They were back home in Jersey within a month.

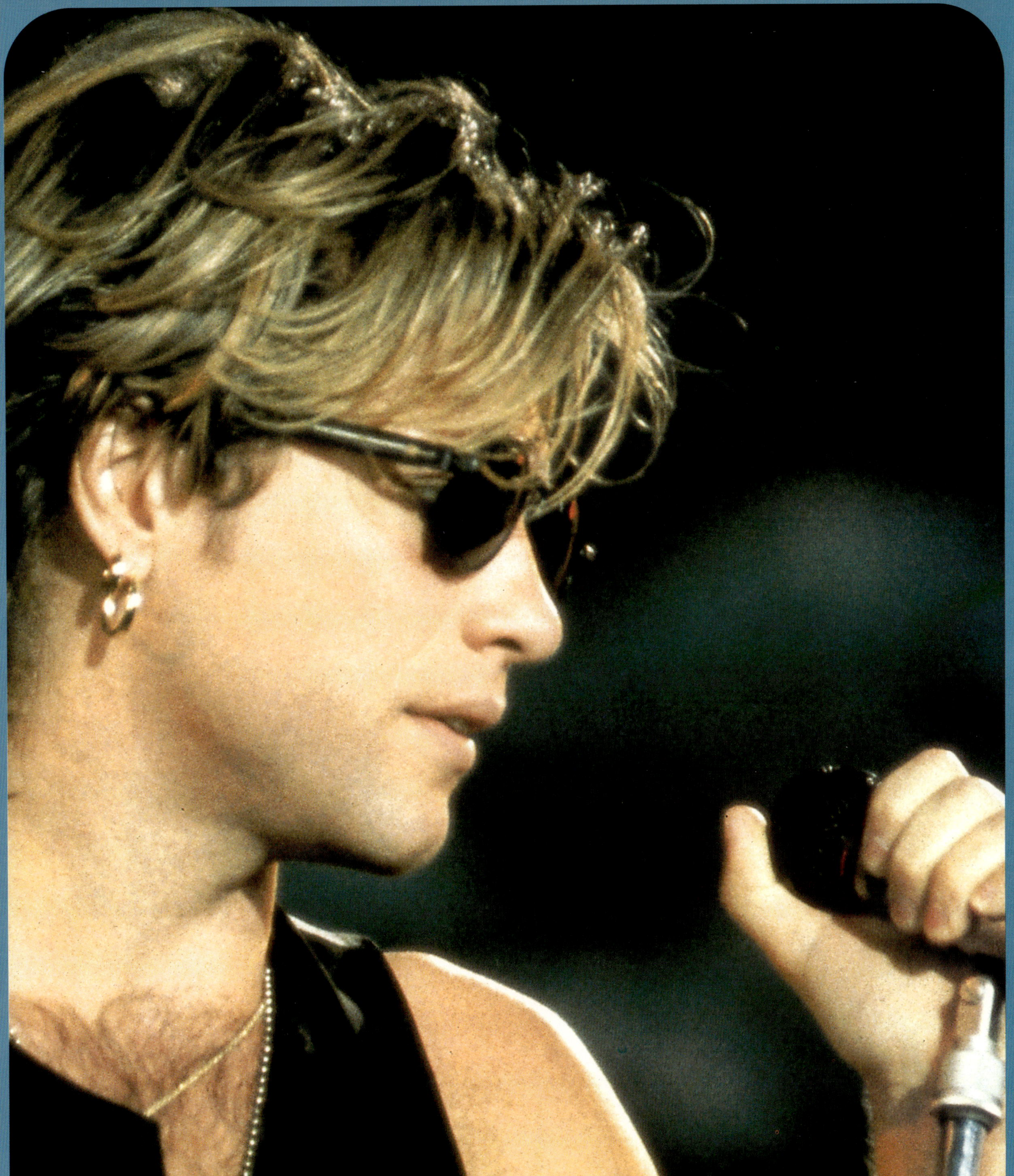

John didn't know where to turn or what to try next. It looked like it was back to square one, even back to the broom. Incredibly, though, a stroke of luck back in New York would finally put John, and David, back on the rails. Power Station assistant engineer Ray Willhard entered The Wild Ones' version of 'Runaway' in a locally-run talent contest called 'From Rock To Riches' organised by radio station WAPP. The track won a regional heat of the contest, and ended up on a compilation album put out by WAPP which was sold locally in the Tri-state area. That did the trick. Suddenly The Wild Ones went from under-the-counter obscurity to the hottest unsigned property on the US east coast.

By early 1983, two major labels were competing for John's signature: Atlantic and PolyGram. And on July 1, 1983 PolyGram landed their man. It was at this point that John became Jon; both in name and in nature. He had already decided to change his name and he also decided to pull out of the final of the 'From Rock To Riches' contest, concentrating instead on putting together a permanent band line-up. 'Bongiovi' could look confusing on a record sleeve or poster; an Americanised 'Bon Jovi' was deemed far more fan-friendly.

After flirting with improbable band names such as Johnny Lightning and Victory, it was suggested by a PolyGram executive that 'Bon Jovi' was the perfect moniker for the group that would back him (Jon was signed primarily as a solo artist to PolyGram). Thus, Rashbaum returned, followed swiftly by drummer Tico Torres, bassist Alec John Such and guitarist Richie Sambora. Jon did toy briefly with the idea of using old school chum Dave Sabo on guitar, but elected instead to go with the more experienced Sambora.

"It was just one of those fated things," Richie would recall years later. "The first time I met Jon, it was just after he'd finished playing this little club date, and I just walked up him to him and told him right out – 'You need me. You're the best frontman I've seen in years and, baby, I'm the best new guitar player there's been for years. We oughta get together!'"

Jon was sceptical at first. But, as he tells it now, "Before we'd even finished the first number we rehearsed together, we knew. The song ended and I just looked at him and said 'Hired!"

Richie was the missing piece of the jigsaw for Jon. Together, they would write some of the most affecting rock anthems of a generation. Pausing only to sign a management deal with the New York-based management company McGhee Entertainment, Bon Jovi took off for their first proper tour together at the tail end of 1983 – a quick round of dates intended to work up new material. Dubbed the 'Stationwagon' Tour, this included a support slot with ZZ Top at Madison Square Garden.

"In some ways it was the best tour we ever did," Jon would later jokingly confess. "Just the band and a small bus and no sleep and no idea if any of it's gonna work. We went out there strangers and came back a real band. Real buddies." They tightened up the new material considerably and improved on the studio demos. Returning from their final date in New York with ZZ Top, they went straight into Power Station to record their first album, with Tony Bongiovi producing, helped by Lance Quinn.

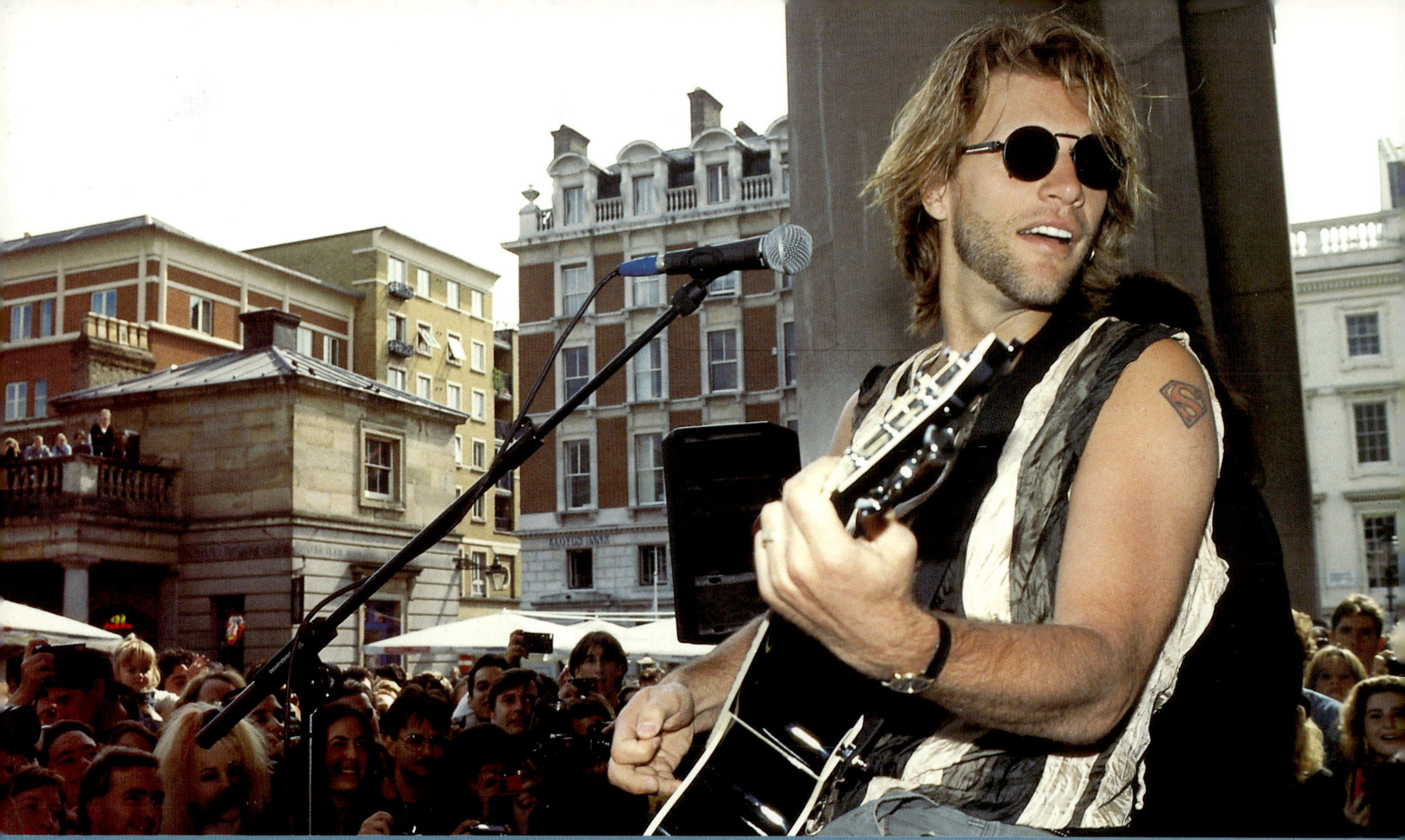

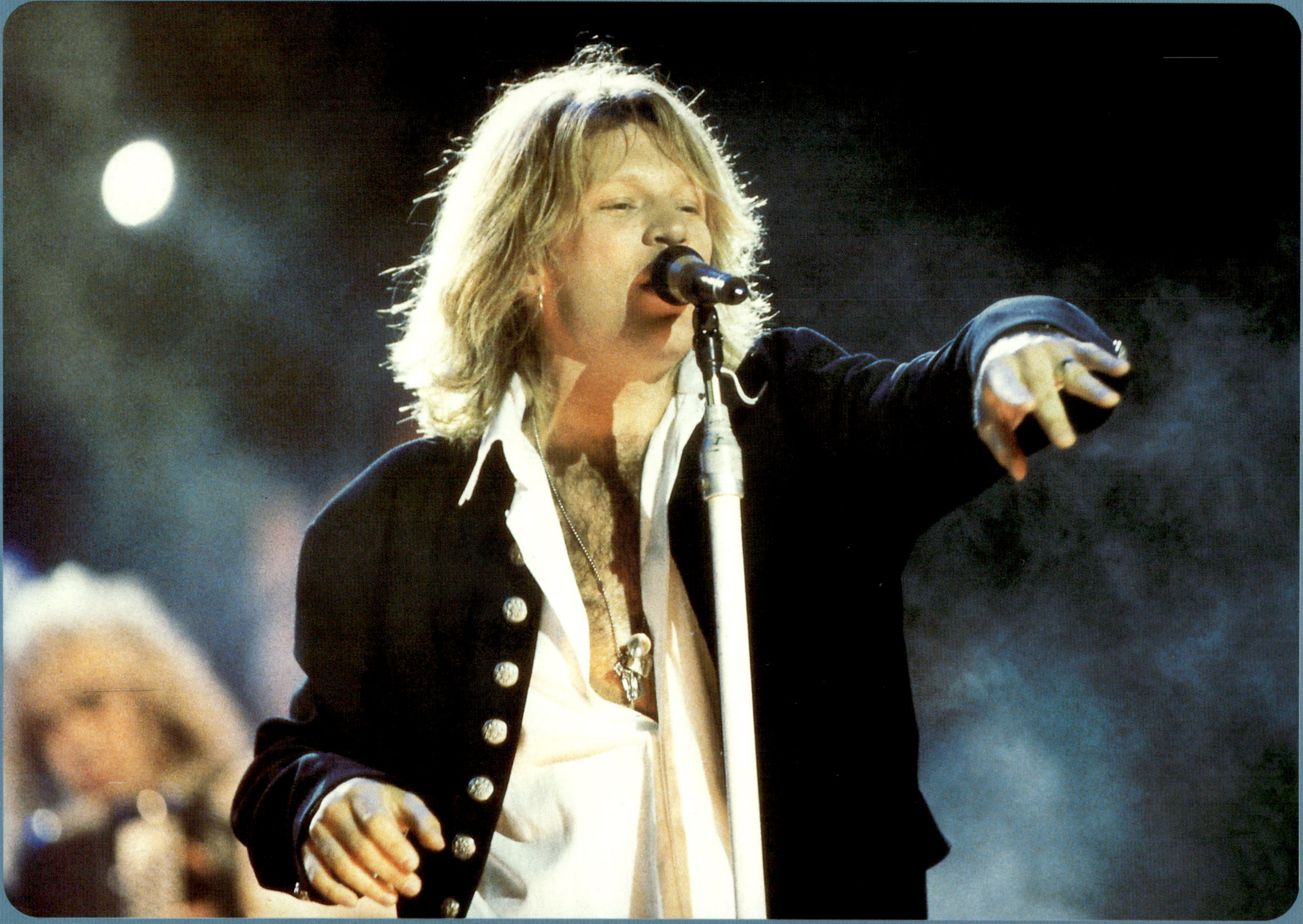

The album, originally to be called 'Tough Talk' but eventually simply 'Bon Jovi', was released in the States during January 1984 and received rave notices; the UK followed suit a few months later. Spurred on by the reasonable success of the single 'Runaway', which reached number 39 in America during February of '84, the 'Bon Jovi' album made it up to number 43 Stateside, racking up decent six-figure sales for a début. British audiences – interest piqued by magazine pictures of the cute lead singer – also pushed the album into the charts, albeit no higher than number 71.

Touring the US in 1984 with The Scorpions, a huge arena-filling act at the time, and the UK and Europe with Kiss, gave the band solid road experience that ensured their fan-base would be firm from the beginning. This, coupled with Jon's natural, all-American good looks and charm, plus songs that were both hard-hitting yet hummable, meant that Bon Jovi were being seen in many quarters as much more than the next bunch of Neanderthal rough-necks ready to break big in hard rock circles. It may have been *Kerrang!* magazine that broke the news of the band in Britain, but with Jon at the front it was only a matter of time before *Smash Hits* got in on the act. Bottom line: Bon Jovi had the potential to be a major force indeed. And much was expected in 1985 of their second album.

The band had undergone one minor and one major change, by the time their second album '7800 Degrees Fahrenheit' was ready to be released in the Spring of 1985. The former saw David Rashbaum change his name to the "less ethnic" David Bryan. However, on a far more significant level, Jon had fallen out with his uncle, Tony Bongiovi, over a disagreement as to how much money the latter was due. The situation got messy, and was finally resolved through legal action. Thus, with uncle Tony and his studio out of the picture, Bon Jovi headed to Philadelphia to work solely with Lance Quinn at The Warehouse Studios on the all-important second album.

These problems, in retrospect, were an omen for the hurried and unsatisfactory way in which that second album would come to fruition. All manner of problems – financial, personal and creative – conspired to ensure that what came out, under the rather mysterious title of '7800 Degrees Fahrenheit' (the temperature at which a volcano will erupt) was a rather dark, occasionally brooding record; not at all what the Bon Jovi public, nor their label, nor the critics, were expecting.

Released in April 1985, '7800 Degrees Fahrenheit' failed to capture the public's imagination on either side of the Atlantic. Still, the album sold well enough in the US to earn the band their first gold disc for sales of over half-a-million copies, and it also breached the Top 40 in America. On the road, the band's reputation was done no harm at all in the States thanks to a support slot on LA band Ratt's arena tour. Ratt were big news at the time in America, and the tour drew the attention of the media wherever it pitched up for the night. Most fans who saw the shows agreed that Bon Jovi were infinitely the better band, displaying a hunger and an edge missing from the performance by more cartoon-like headliners.

In Europe the Jovis had by now reached head-lining status in their own right, albeit at a lower level. But they could still fill theatres, supported by Canadian singer Lee Aaron. And, if '7800 Degrees Fahrenheit' wasn't the huge commercial triumph many had expected, the band had made vast strides, as was seen in the UK during August 1985, when Bon Jovi appeared third on the bill at the Castle Donington Monsters Of Rock Festival. It was a prestigious moment for Jon and the band, with headliners ZZ Top and Marillion above them on the bill, and Metallica, Ratt and Magnum coming before them.

Again, most of the talk after the festival was about the enormous impression made by Bon Jovi. '7800 Degrees Fahrenheit' may have been an artistic dud but live the band was better than ever.

"That first time at Donington, I was like a little kid let loose in a candy store," Jon later confided. "We had read so much about Donington and then to actually be there... you know, it's funny, because I actually remember our first appearance at Donington much better than I remember when we went back there two years later and actually headlined the show. That was such a part of the huge mad rush that followed 'Slippery When Wet' and I was so fried by the time we got there, I hardly remember that at all. But that first time. Now that was different... "

A month earlier in the States, Bon Jovi had appeared at the high profile Farm Aid charity festival in Montana, organised by John Cougar Mellencamp and Willie Nelson. They performed before 83,000 fans, plus millions more on TV, and played a new song written specially for the occasion called 'Heart Of America'. It was more proof, if such were needed, that the band were making slow, steady progress. But what they really required was a hefty launch to a new level.

They were under considerable pressure from PolyGram and it was even rumoured at one point that the higher-ups at the label, disappointed at the sales figures for the second Bon Jovi album, were seriously contemplating dropping the band from their roster. It was necessary for Bon Jovi to revamp their approach for the recording of their make-or-break third album.

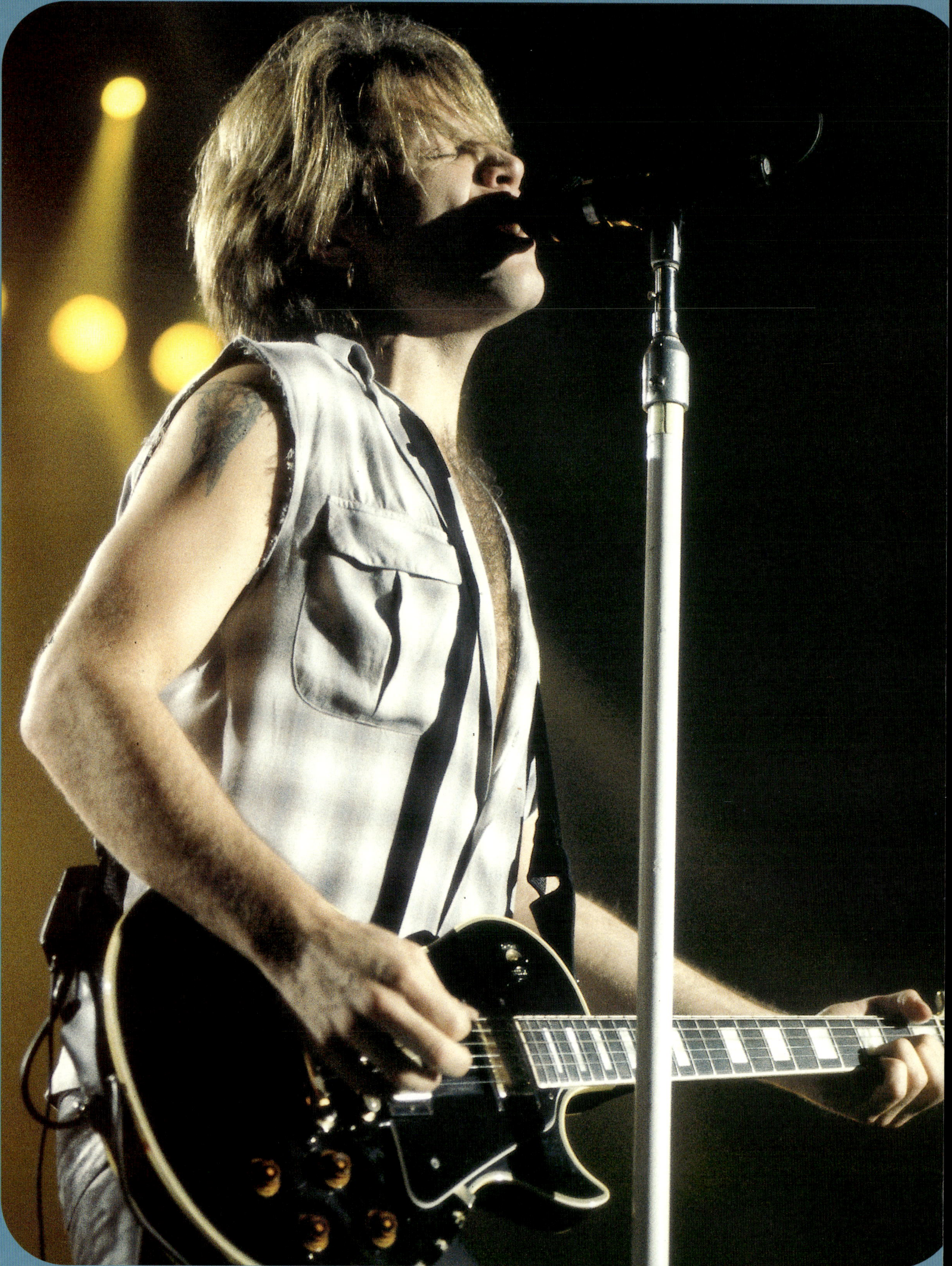

This time, nothing would be left to chance. Selected songs – the ones that would eventually end up as singles, in most cases – were co-written with LA songsmith Desmond Child, and the band relocated to Little Mountain Studios in Vancouver to record them with renowned Canadian producer Bruce Fairbairn. The result? A state-of-the-art pop-rock album designed to take the world's unsuspecting charts by storm.

'Slippery When Wet', the third Bon Jovi album, was destined to become one of the all-time great rock albums – an all-time best seller that boasted some of the most memorable rock songs of the Eighties. Released in August 1986, it quickly became obvious that 'Slippery When Wet' would be a massive hit. Ultimately, the album has gone on to sell more than 18 million copies world-wide, topped the US charts twice, reached number six in the UK, and spawned two US number one singles in 'You Give Love A Bad Name' and 'Livin' On A Prayer', as well as the unforgettably panoramic 'Wanted: Dead Or Alive'.

"It's one of those very few rock albums that you can play pretty much every track from on the radio," says Trevor White, head of programming at Virgin Radio. "Tracks like 'Wanted: Dead Or Alive' simply never go out of fashion. Almost every track was a late-Eighties classic." And, with Jon's matinee idol good looks getting the band press coverage way beyond the rock spectrum, and the band committed to a gruelling 17-month long world tour, Bon Jovi rapidly became a household name across the globe throughout the tail-end of 1986 and 1987. Rock fans, who had been following the band since that first album, still saw them as essentially 'their band', but now they were attracting legions of fans - in particular, girls more used to watching their favourite singers on *Top Of The Pops* than going out to sweaty gigs.

Ironically, when 'Slippery When Wet' first started breaking big, the band were out on the road in the States, supporting ageing southern rockers .38 Special. "I'll never forget the night [band manager] Doc told me on the phone that 'You Give Love A Bad Name' had gone to number one," Jon recalled with a distant smile one night years later. "I was standing in the hall backstage at a gig with .38 Special. We were just about to go on and I was standing there talking to Doc on a pay-phone. And he said, 'Congratulations, you've just gone to number one!'"

Inevitably, the sudden and, from here on in, seemingly unstoppable momentum of 'Slippery When Wet' forced the band to abandon plans for more support slots and go out on their own as major headliners for the first time, selling out tour after tour across the globe.

Jon's intense work ethic kept Bon Jovi playing live throughout 1986 and 1987, almost driving them into the ground. But the demand for Bon Jovi was overwhelming. And arguably the highlight of this period came in August 1987 when the Jovis returned to Donington to headline the annual Castle Donington Monsters Of Rock Festival, the most prestigious date on the British rock calendar, just two years after appearing third on the bill. The day was a huge triumph for Jon and the boys; their set was the climax to a day that also saw Dio, Metallica, Anthrax, W.A.S.P. and Bon Jovi protégés Cinderella performing before more than 80,000 fans, one of the largest crowds the festival has ever drawn.

In all, Bon Jovi played nearly 200 shows over 16 months on the 'Slippery...' tour, grossing nearly $30 million. So, by the end of the summer of '87, they were ready for a lengthy and well-earned rest, right? Wrong. By Christmas of that year, Jon and Richie had already amassed a pile of songs for a new album, and early in 1988 the band were told to pack their bags and get ready for another album-length stay in Vancouver. "Rest is just something else other people do," says Jon. "I've never been able to switch off for long periods of time. For me, life is about doing, not waiting to do."

Once again working with Bruce Fairbairn at Little Mountain Studios, the original plan was for the Jovis to record a double album called 'Sons Of Beaches'. A sleeve based on that title was even mocked up. But eventually, almost certainly at the insistence of management, the plans were changed. 'Sons Of Beaches' became 'New Jersey', a single, much more commercially viable, album released in October 1988.

It was an enormous success, reaching the top of the charts on both sides of the Atlantic, and songs such as 'Bad Medicine', the first single, soon became an important part of the Bon Jovi live experience. Showing an almost limitless capacity for work, they undertook a lengthy tour that lasted another 16 months, some 237 shows. Highlights included a headlining appearance at Giants Stadium in their home state of New Jersey, a sure sign of success. In support was none other than old friend Billy Squier, whom the Jovis had once supported and who, of course, produced a very early demo for Jon.

In August 1989 the band played an outdoor show in the UK at the Milton Keynes Bowl, headlining a bill that also featured Europe, all-girl band Vixen and another act just taken under the Jovi wing, Skid Row, who featured Jon's old guitar-wielding school pal and former band-mate, Dave 'Snake' Sabo. Bon Jovi had hoped to play the prestigious Wembley Stadium that day, but Bros had already booked the venue. So Milton Keynes it was and what a day! At the end, Steven Tyler and Joe Perry, singer and guitarist, respectively, of Aerosmith, joined Jon and the band on stage for a blistering run-through of the old R&B classic, 'Train Kept A-Rollin''. With Donington cancelled that year (it would be back in 1990), Milton Keynes is remembered in the UK as the best outdoor rock event of 1989.

1989 was to prove an eventful year for the band in other, unforeseen, ways. Jon finally married childhood sweetheart Dorothea Hurley on April 29, in Las Vegas, and on the weekend of August 12 and 13, the band headlined two special shows in Moscow, appearing before some 70,000 people at the Olympic Lenin Stadium. The shows were billed as the Moscow Music Peace Festival, an event organised by Jovi manager Doc McGhee as part of his sentence for being convicted of smuggling a huge quantity of drugs into the States several years before. As part of his punishment, McGhee had been ordered to set up the 'Make A Difference Foundation', an organisation dedicated to combating drug and alcohol abuse problems, specifically among the young. An album called 'Stairway To Heaven/Highway To Hell' would later emerge, featuring contemporary bands covering songs associated with artists who had died because of drug-related incidents. Bon Jovi covered Thin Lizzy's 'The Boys Are Back In Town', Jon being a major fan of the late Lizzy bassist/vocalist Phil Lynott, who died in December 1985 from complications brought on by a life-time of drug abuse.

But the shows in Moscow, for all their ostensible goodwill, proved to be something of a public relations disaster. Arguments ensued almost from the moment the bands - including the Jovis, Motley Crue, Ozzy Osbourne, Skid Row, The Scorpions and Cinderella - landed in Russia. Officially, whilst Bon Jovi would close the show on both nights, they were not the actual headliners; nobody was. But when it was discovered that Bon Jovi would be the only band using fireworks to enhance their show, there was dissent in the ranks. Motley Crue, still huge stars in America at that time, were already upset by their comparatively low place on the bill, and they grew openly more recalcitrant as show time approached. The outcome was a fist fight at the side of the stage between Motley drummer Tommy Lee (better known perhaps as Mr Pamela Anderson) and Doc McGhee, who also managed the Crue at this time. Shortly afterwards, Motley - none too surprisingly - parted company with the Doc.

Overall, though, the 'New Jersey' period had augmented Bon Jovi's place as the premier hard rock band on the planet. But by the beginning of 1990, the five-piece were in danger of burning out from their exhausting schedule. It was time for a lengthy break.

Jon, of course, soon grew bored with that idea. A self-confessed workaholic, he decided to take up an offer to write the soundtrack for Hollywood Brat Pack cowboy movie *Young Guns II*, starring Emilio Estevez, Keifer Sutherland and Lou Diamond Phillips. Writing all the material himself, Jon didn't call up anyone from Bon Jovi to play on the record. West Coast session veteran Danny Kortchmar was co-producer, and Jon indulged his musical fantasies, inviting Jeff Beck, Elton John and Little Richard, amongst others, to play on the album.

The soundtrack for *Young Guns II* came out during the summer of 1990, to much high-profile acclaim. It rapidly racked up major sales figures, topping the two million mark in the States alone. The song 'Blaze Of Glory' was voted 'Best Original Song' at the 1990 Golden Globe film awards, as well as 'Best Pop/Rock single' at the 1991 American Music Awards, when Jon performed it accompanied by Richie and a posse of session guys. 'Blaze Of Glory' was even nominated in the 'Best Original Song In A Film' category at the Academy Awards, although Jon was pipped at the post for this one.

Jon also announced plans for his own label, originally to be called Underground, but finally titled Jambco. First signings were folk rocker Bill Falcon and one-time Canadian superstar Aldo Nova, another old buddy of Jon's who had fallen on hard times. This was seen by many as Jon repaying a favour since Aldo had appeared on the first Bon Jovi album, at a time when his stock was enormously high. Now, when Aldo needed a helping hand, Jon was there for him, helping to write and record an album that would be called 'Blood On The Bricks', coming out in 1991, as did the début album from Falcon. Sadly, though, neither record made any commercial impact – although both did garner some critical favour – and the Jambco label quickly became the new home solely for Bon Jovi and associated projects.

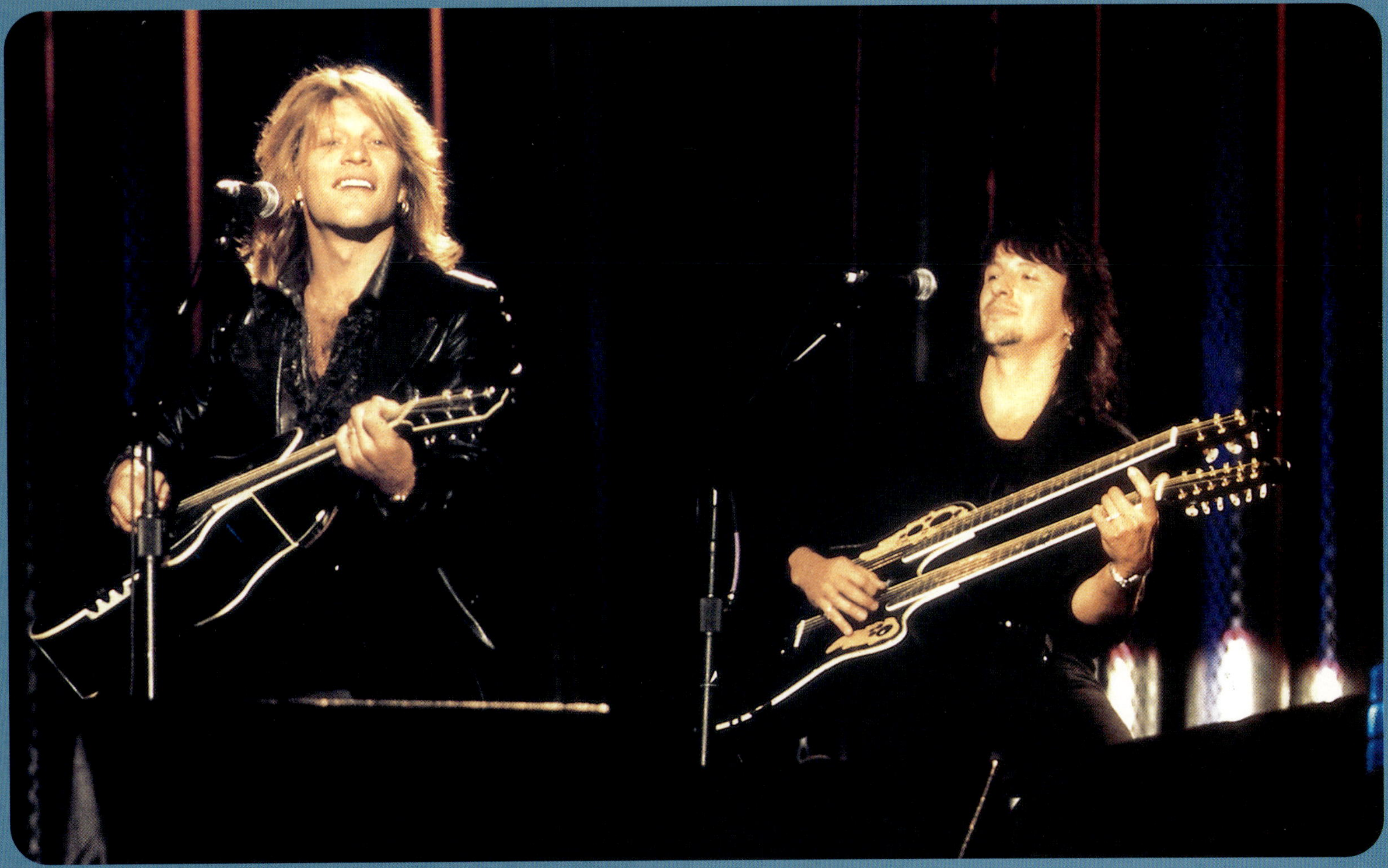

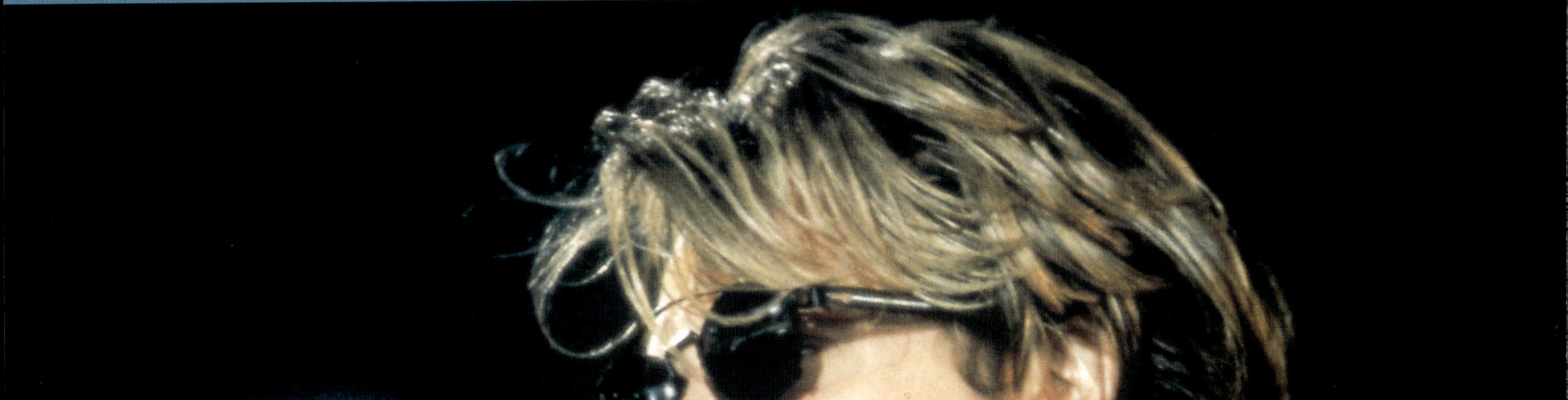

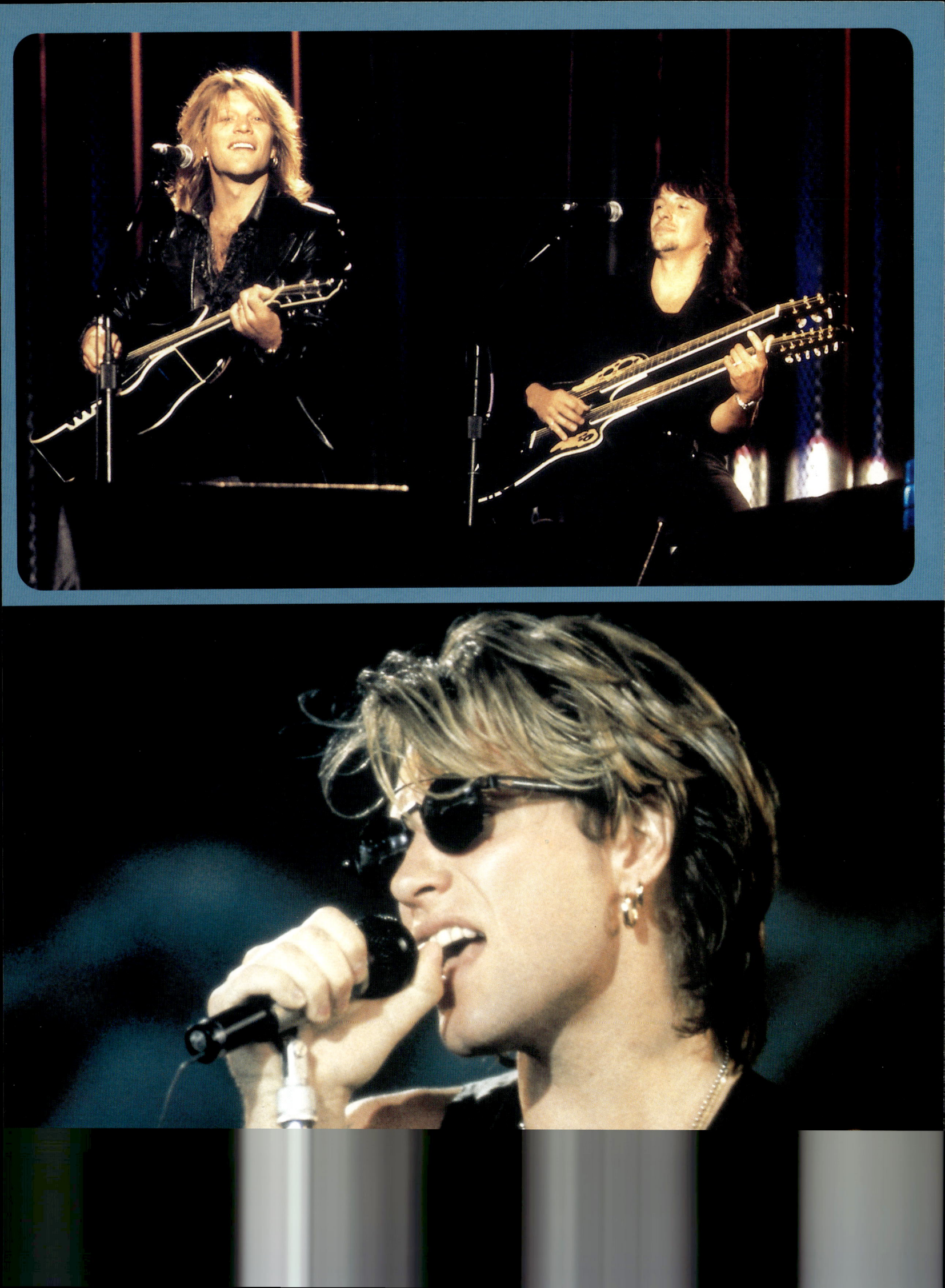

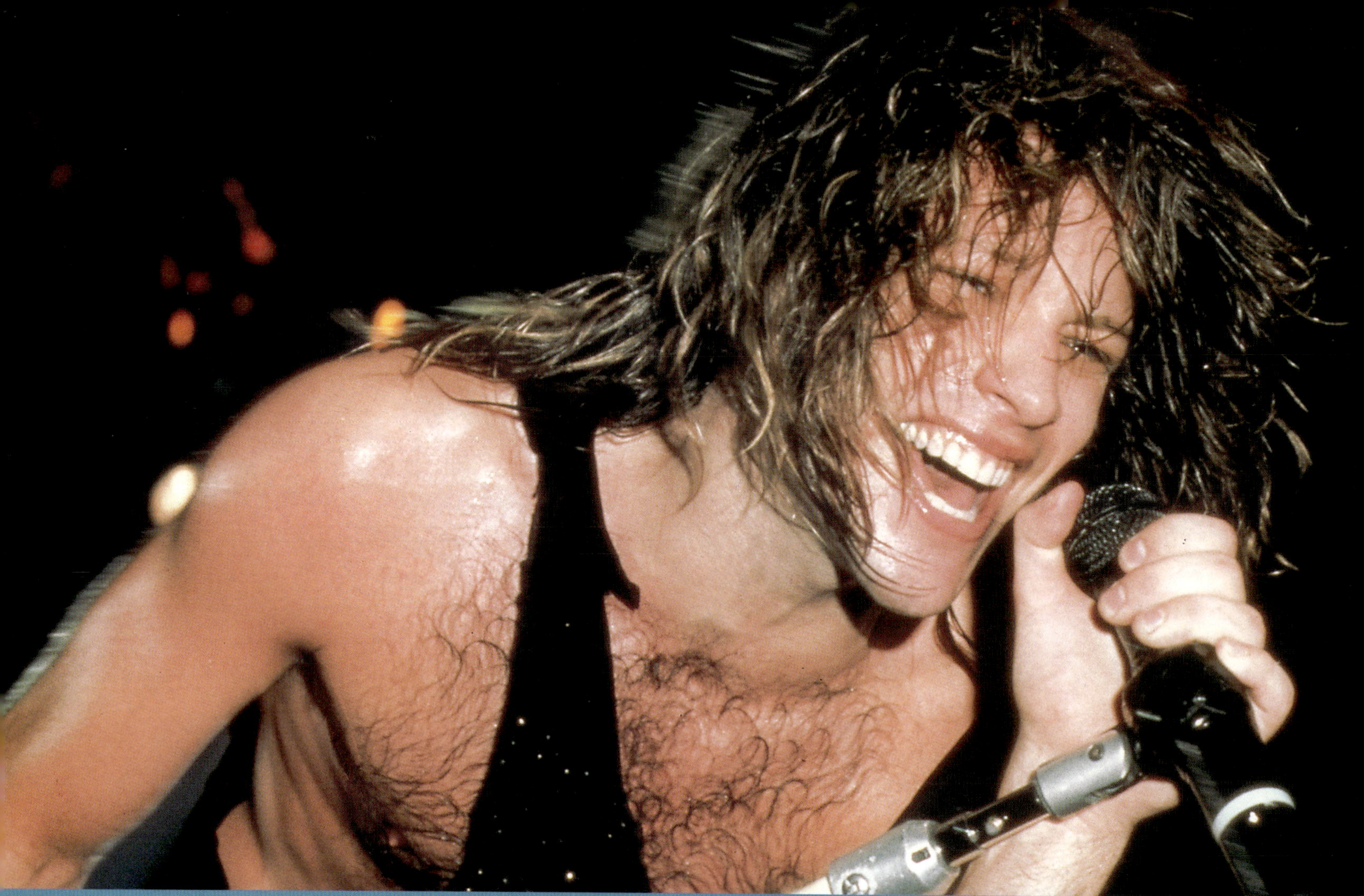

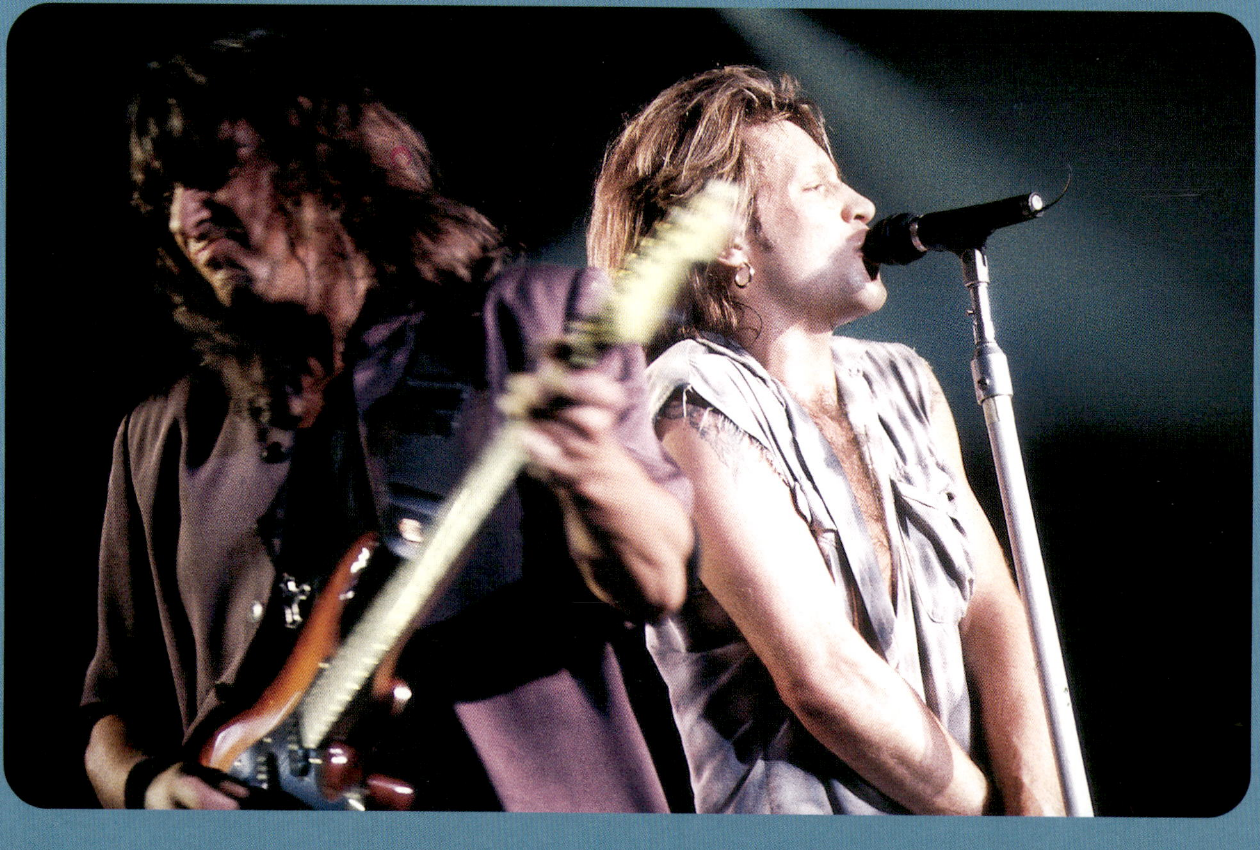

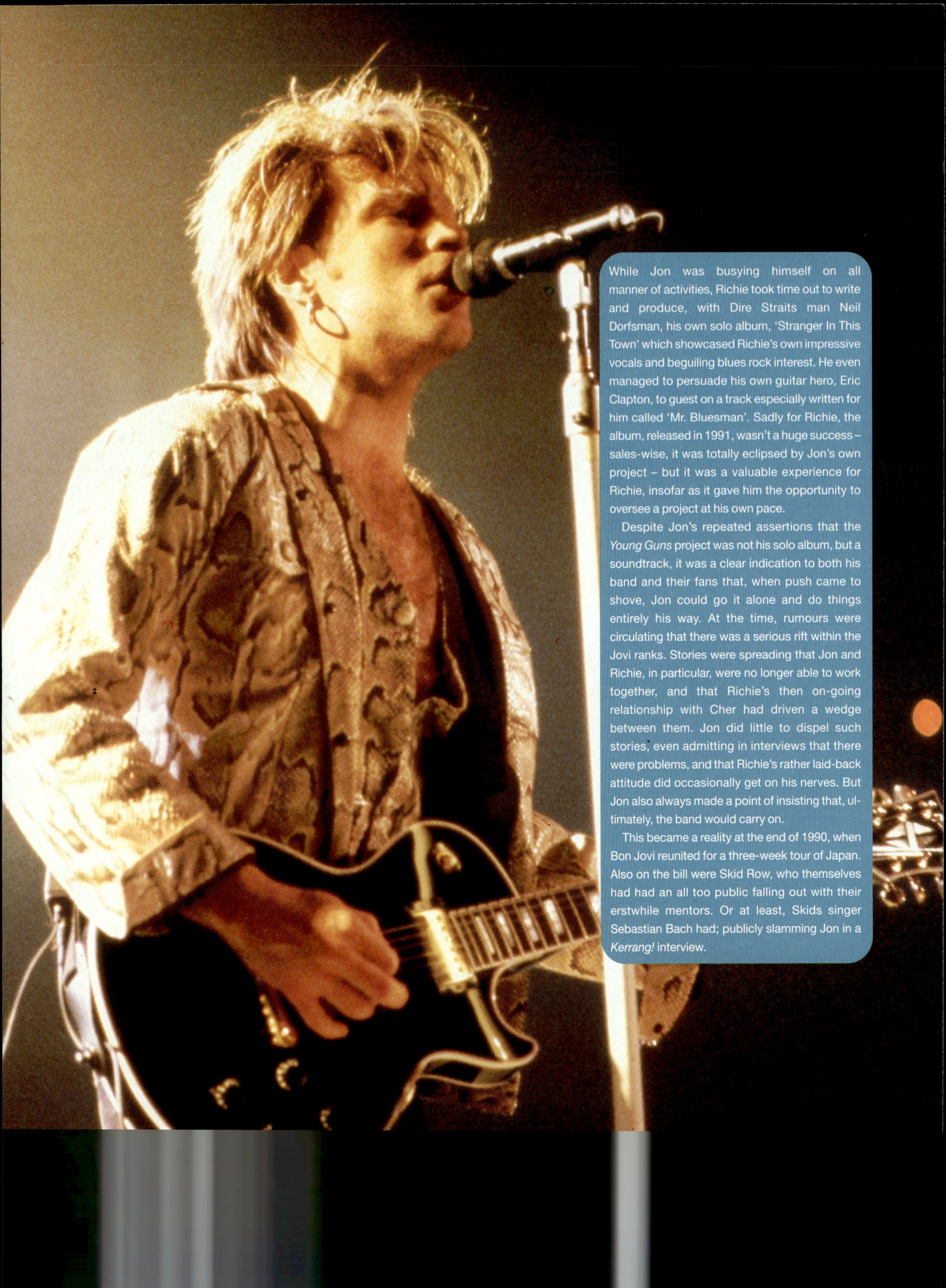

While Jon was busying himself on all manner of activities, Richie took time out to write and produce, with Dire Straits man Neil Dorfsman, his own solo album, 'Stranger In This Town' which showcased Richie's own impressive vocals and beguiling blues rock interest. He even managed to persuade his own guitar hero, Eric Clapton, to guest on a track especially written for him called 'Mr. Bluesman'. Sadly for Richie, the album, released in 1991, wasn't a huge success – sales-wise, it was totally eclipsed by Jon's own project – but it was a valuable experience for Richie, insofar as it gave him the opportunity to oversee a project at his own pace.

Despite Jon's repeated assertions that the *Young Guns* project was not his solo album, but a soundtrack, it was a clear indication to both his band and their fans that, when push came to shove, Jon could go it alone and do things entirely his way. At the time, rumours were circulating that there was a serious rift within the Jovi ranks. Stories were spreading that Jon and Richie, in particular, were no longer able to work together, and that Richie's then on-going relationship with Cher had driven a wedge between them. Jon did little to dispel such stories, even admitting in interviews that there were problems, and that Richie's rather laid-back attitude did occasionally get on his nerves. But Jon also always made a point of insisting that, ultimately, the band would carry on.

This became a reality at the end of 1990, when Bon Jovi reunited for a three-week tour of Japan. Also on the bill were Skid Row, who themselves had had an all too public falling out with their erstwhile mentors. Or at least, Skids singer Sebastian Bach had; publicly slamming Jon in a *Kerrang!* interview.

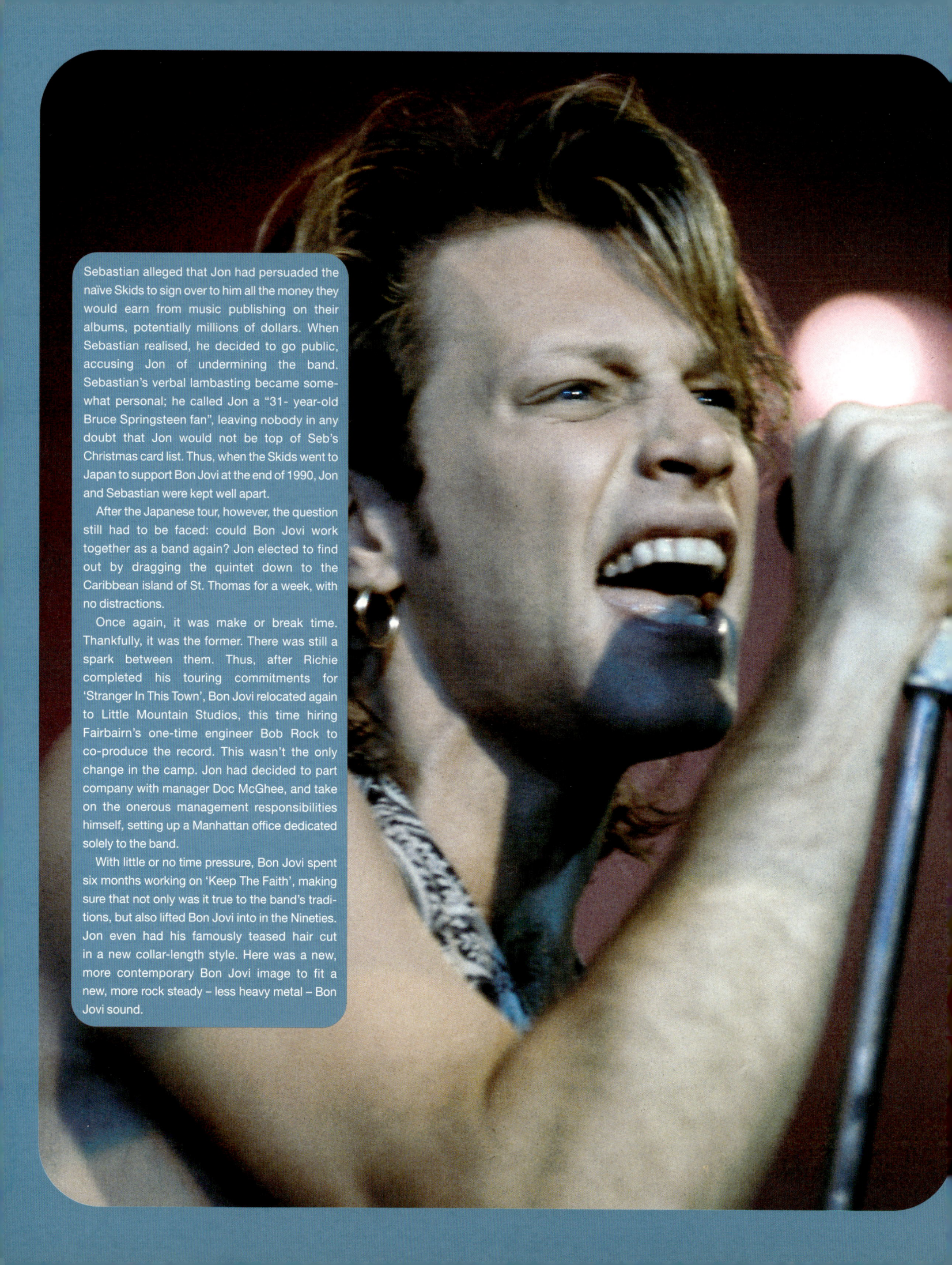

Sebastian alleged that Jon had persuaded the naïve Skids to sign over to him all the money they would earn from music publishing on their albums, potentially millions of dollars. When Sebastian realised, he decided to go public, accusing Jon of undermining the band. Sebastian's verbal lambasting became somewhat personal; he called Jon a "31- year-old Bruce Springsteen fan", leaving nobody in any doubt that Jon would not be top of Seb's Christmas card list. Thus, when the Skids went to Japan to support Bon Jovi at the end of 1990, Jon and Sebastian were kept well apart.

After the Japanese tour, however, the question still had to be faced: could Bon Jovi work together as a band again? Jon elected to find out by dragging the quintet down to the Caribbean island of St. Thomas for a week, with no distractions.

Once again, it was make or break time. Thankfully, it was the former. There was still a spark between them. Thus, after Richie completed his touring commitments for 'Stranger In This Town', Bon Jovi relocated again to Little Mountain Studios, this time hiring Fairbairn's one-time engineer Bob Rock to co-produce the record. This wasn't the only change in the camp. Jon had decided to part company with manager Doc McGhee, and take on the onerous management responsibilities himself, setting up a Manhattan office dedicated solely to the band.

With little or no time pressure, Bon Jovi spent six months working on 'Keep The Faith', making sure that not only was it true to the band's traditions, but also lifted Bon Jovi into in the Nineties. Jon even had his famously teased hair cut in a new collar-length style. Here was a new, more contemporary Bon Jovi image to fit a new, more rock steady – less heavy metal – Bon Jovi sound.

It worked. Released in October 1992, the album sold hugely in the UK and US, and the usual bout of intense roadwork over the next year or so underscored the band's newly-won reputation as an international act to be mentioned in the same breath as The Rolling Stones, Bruce Springsteen and U2. No longer 'merely' a huge rock band, the Jovis were now perennials. Though their stock in the States had fallen somewhat, in Europe the band were bigger than ever.

Their huge success in the UK continued apace, with two sell-out dates at the Milton Keynes Bowl during September 1993, with the Manic Street Preachers, Billy Idol and Little Angels backing them up. This was further augmented when, in January 1994, Jon, Richie and Tico flew over to England to perform live at the Brits along with soul-diva Dinah Carroll. Jon and Richie also recorded a version of the George Gershwin number 'How Long Has This Been Going On' with one-time Beatles producer George Martin. This was for inclusion on a tribute album to harmonica great Larry Adler.

The absence of both David Bryan and Alec John Such at the Brits caused some consternation (Aldo Nova stepped in for Bryan and former Meat Loaf/Utopia man Kasim Sultan took over from Such). David couldn't make it over because his wife had just given birth to twins, but Alec? His non-appearance was side-stepped by Bon Jovi, giving rise to rumours that he was on his way out of the band, and this was confirmed with the passage of time.

In October 1994, Bon Jovi unleashed a greatest hits package called 'Cross Road'. It was to prove an enormous success, selling more than a million copies in the UK alone, and in the process becoming the biggest selling album of the year in Britain – bar none. The album, which hit the top spot in both Britain and the States, featured two new tracks: 'Always', released as a single, and a huge hit, reaching number two in Britain and number four in the US, and 'Someday I'll Be Saturday Night', both produced by Englishman Peter Collins.

Jon and Richie came over to London during September to promote the 'Always' single and the 'Cross Road' album. They made a surprise appearance at The Piazza in Covent Garden, busking before 3,000 fans. The duo performed sit-down acoustic versions of both 'Always' and 'Someday I'll Be Saturday Night', a new version of 'Livin' On A Prayer' (called 'Prayer '94'), 'Wanted Dead Or Alive' and a cover of the Paul Simon standard, 'Bridge Over Troubled Water'.

While over in the UK, Jon announced plans to appear in a major film role for the first time, playing the male lead in the movie *Moonlight & Valentino* opposite Whoopi Goldberg, Elizabeth Perkins and Katherine Turner. And in December 1994, Jon appeared in a promotional video for the Bon Jovi single 'Please Come Home For Christmas' with supermodel Cindy Crawford. The song was originally a Jon Bon Jovi solo effort recorded for the charity record 'A Very Special Christmas II', all proceeds from which went to the Special Olympics.

By the end of '94, Bon Jovi were busy working on their next record at Bearsville Studios in Upstate New York with Peter Collins. By this time, Richie had married soap star Heather Locklear, previously married to Motley Crue's Tommy Lee, in Paris.

Alec John Such was still nowhere in sight. Was he out of the band? All anyone connected with the Jovis would say was that session man Hugh MacDonald was with them in the studio, but that Alec might still tour with the band in the Summer of '95, when they were due to undertake yet another hectic stadium tour of Europe.

By the time Bon Jovi hit the road in the Spring of '95, their new album 'These Days' was in the shops and selling well everywhere. Further proof, if any were needed, that this band weren't dependent on trends or the transient patronage of critics. The band's UK tour included no less than three nights at Wembley Stadium, equalling the Stones' record-breaking run that same summer. It was an amazing testament to the Jovis that they could achieve such a run. And who was on bass? None other than Hugh MacDonald. Alec John Such was finally confirmed as a former member of Bon Jovi – the first line-up change the band had undergone in a decade. Officially, it was said that Alec had left the band of his own volition, but Jon has always been very tight-lipped on the subject.

Nevertheless, with or without Alec, Bon Jovis' exhilarating performances on the tour left no-one in any doubt that they were still a potent force. Not content just to tour Europe once on the back of 'These Days', Bon Jovi quickly announced further outdoor dates for July 1996. This allowed time for Jon to spend the first part of the year in London filming his second major movie role in *The Leading Man*. He was also being linked with a big part in *City Of Angels*, the sequel to the highly acclaimed *The Crow*. What's more, Jon also found time to become the new celebrity model for Italian fashion giant Gianni Versace; his first assignment took him to Argentina, where he was photographed performing dressed as a cowboy. He also turned up at the Sky Sports' Champions Of Sport awards ceremony to accept an award on behalf of the Special Olympics, with whom he has worked closely.

In between all of this activity, Jon had also somehow found time for his family; he's the proud father of two children. During the first part of 1996 Richie took the opportunity to work on a second solo album, while Tico relaxed with model girlfriend Eva 'Wonder bra' Herzegova and David worked on some solo ideas of his own.

But come the summer of 1996, Bon Jovi are back together, ready to rock the world again. It's been a long journey from the streets of New Jersey to picking up the award for Best International Group at the 1996 Brits ceremony in London last February, but Jon and Bon Jovi are now at the very pinnacle of their profession.

The future? Maybe they'll split up before the millennium. More likely, though, they'll celebrate this momentous occasion in some very special manner. Besides, the year 2000 will be the 20th anniversary of Jon's employment at The Power Station, which started him on the long road towards becoming the superstar he is today.

Don't bet against there being a Bon Jovi party somewhere that night ...

BON JOVI – DISCOGRAPHY

SINGLES

She Don't Know Me/Breakout
(VERTIGO VER 11 – MAY 1984)
She Don't Know Me/Breakout
(VERTIGO VERX 11 – MAY 1984)
Runaway/Breakout (live)
(VERTIGO VER14 – OCTOBER 1984)
Runaway/Breakout (live)/Runaway (live)
(VERTIGO VERX14 – OCTOBER 1984)
In And Out Of Love/Roulette (live)
(VERTIGO VER 19 – MAY 1985)
In And Out Of Love/Roulette (live)
(VERTIGO VERP 19 PICTURE DISC – MAY 1985)
In And Out Of Love/Roulette (live)/Shot Through The Heart (live)
(VERTIGO VERX 19 – MAY 1985)
The Hardest Part Is The Night/Always Run To You
(VERTIGO VER 22 – AUGUST 1985)
The Hardest Part Is The Night/Always Run To You/Tokyo Road (live)
(VERTIGO VERX 22 – AUGUST 1985)
The Hardest Part Is The Night/Always Run To You/Tokyo Road (live)/Shot Through The Heart (live)
(VERTIGO VERDP 22 – AUGUST 1985)
The Hardest Part Is The Night/Tokyo Road (live)/In And Out Of Love (live)
(VERTIGO VERXR 22 – AUGUST 1985)
You Give Love A Bad Name/Let It Rock
(VERTIGO VER26 – AUGUST 1986)
You Give Love A Bad Name/Let It Rock
(VERTIGO VERP 26 PICTURE DISC – AUGUST 1986)
You Give Love A Bad Name/Let It Rock/Borderline
(VERTIGO VERX 26 – AUGUST 1986)
You Give Love A Bad Name/Let It Rock/The Hardest Part Is The Night (live)/Burning For Love (live)
(VERTIGO VERXR 26 BLUE VINYL – AUGUST 1986)
Living On A Prayer/Wild In The Streets
(VERTIGO VER 29 – OCTOBER 1986)
Living On A Prayer/Wild In The Streets/Edge Of A Broken Heart
(VERTIGO VERXP 28 GREEN VINYL – NOVEMBER 1986)
Living On A Prayer/Wild In The Streets
(VERTIGO VERPA 28 WITH FREE SEW-ON PATCH – NOVEMBER 1986)
Living On A Prayer/Wild In The Streets
(VERTIGO VERP 28 PICTURE DISC – NOVEMBER 1986)
Living On A Prayer/Wild In The Streets/Only Love (live)/Runaway (live)
(VERTIGO VERXG 28 – NOVEMBER 1986)
Wanted: Dead Or Alive/Shot Through The Heart
(VERTIGO JOV 1 – MARCH 1987)
Wanted: Dead Or Alive/Shot Through The Heart/Social Disease
(VERTIGO JOV112 – MARCH 1987)
Wanted: Dead Or Alive/Shot Through The Heart
(VERTIGO JOVS 1 WITH FREE STICKER – MARCH 1987)
Wanted: Dead Or Alive/Shot Through The Heart/Social Disease/Get Ready (live)
(VERTIGO JOVR 112 SILVER VINYL – APRIL 1987)
Never Say Goodbye/Raise Your Hands
(VERTIGO JOV 2 – AUGUST 1987)
Never Say Goodbye/Raise Your Hands/Wanted: Dead Or Alive (acoustic)
(VERTIGO JOV 212 – AUGUST 1987)
Never Say Goodbye/Raise Your Hands/Wanted: Dead Or Alive (acoustic)
(VERTIGO JOVR 212 YELLOW VINYL – AUGUST 1987)
Never Say Goodbye/Raise Your Hands
(VERTIGO JOVC 2 CASSETTE SINGLE – AUGUST 1987)
Bad Medicine/99 In The Shade
(VERTIGO JOV 3 – SEPTEMBER 1988)
Bad Medicine/99 In The Shade/Lay Your Hand On Me
(VERTIGO JOV 312 – SEPTEMBER 1988)
Bad Medicine/99 In The Shade
(VERTIGO JOVCD 3 CD SINGLE – SEPTEMBER 1988)
Bad Medicine/99 In The Shade
(VERTIGO JOVR 3 WRAP-AROUND SLEEVE – SEPTEMBER 1988)
Bad Medicine/You Give Love A Bad
(VERTIGO JOVR 312 – SEPTEMBER 1988)
Born To Be My Baby/Love For Sale
(VERTIGO JOV 4 – NOVEMBER 1988)
Born To Be My Baby/Love For Sale/Wanted: Dead Or Alive
(VERTIGO JOV 412 – NOVEMBER 1988)
Born To Be My Baby/Love For Sale/Runaway (live)/Living On A Prayer (live)
(VERTIGO JOVCD 4 CD SINGLE – NOVEMBER 1988)
I'll Be There For You/Homebound Train
(VERTIGO JOV 5 – APRIL 1989)
I'll Be There For You/Homebound Train/Wild In The Streets (live)
(VERTIGO JOV 512 – APRIL 1989)
I'll Be There For You/Homebound Train/Wild In The Streets
(VERTIGO JOVR 512 POSTER SLEEVE – APRIL 1989)
I'll Be There For You/Homebound Train/Borderline (live)/Edge Of A Broken Heart (live)
(VERTIGO JOVCD 5 CD SINGLE – APRIL 1989)
Lay Your Hands On Me/Bad Medicine (live)
(VERTIGO JOV 661 RED VINYL – AUGUST 1989)
Lay Your Hands On Me/Bad Medicine (live)
(VERTIGO JOV 662 WHITE VINYL – AUGUST 1989)
Lay Your Hands On Me/Bad Medicine (live)
(VERTIGO JOV 663 BLUE VINYL – AUGUST 1989)
Lay Your Hands On Me/Bad Medicine
(VERTIGO JOV 610 SHAPED PICTURE DISC – AUGUST 1989)
Lay Your Hands On Me/Bad Medicine (live)/Blood On Blood (live)
(VERTIGO JOV 612 – AUGUST 1989)
Lay Your Hands On Me/Bad Medicine (live)/Blood On Blood (live)
(VERTIGO JOVCD 6 CD SINGLE – AUGUST 1989)
Living In Sin/Love Is War
(VERTIGO JOV 7 - NOVEMBER 1989)
Living In Sin/Love Is War/Ride Cowboy Ride
(VERTIGO JOV712 - NOVEMBER 1989)
Blaze Of Glory/You Really Got Me Now
(JAMBCO JBJ 1 - JULY 1990)
Blaze Of Glory/You Really Got Me Now/Blood Money
(JAMBCO JBJ 112 - JULY 1990)
Blaze Of Glory/You Really Got Me Now
(JAMBCO JBJMC1 - JULY 1990)

Blood Money
(JAMBCO JBJ CD 1 - JULY 1990)
Miracle/Bang A Drum
(JAMBCO JBJ 2 - OCTOBER 1990)
Miracle/Dyin' Ain't Much Of A Livin'/Interview
(JAMBCO JBJ 212 - OCTOBER 1990)
Miracle/Bang A Drum
(JAMBCO JBJ MC2 - OCTOBER 1990)
Miracle/Dyin' Ain't Much Of A Livin'/Going Back (live)
(JAMBCO JBJ CD 2 - OCTOBER 1990)
Miracle/Dyin' Ain't Much Of A Livin'/Going Back (live)
(JAMBCO JBJP 212 - OCTOBER 1990)
Keep The Faith/I Wish Everyday Could Be Like Christmas
(JAMBCO JOV 8 - OCTOBER 1992)
Keep The Faith/I Wish Everyday Could Be Like Christmas
(JAMBCO JOVMC 8 - OCTOBER 1992)
Keep The Faith/I Wish Everyday Could Be Like Christmas/Little Bit Of Soul
(JAMBCO JOV CD 8 - OCTOBER 1992)
Keep The Faith/I Wish Everyday Could Be Like Christmas/Living In Sin (live)
(JAMBCO JOV CB 8 - OCTOBER 1992)
Bed Of Roses/Starting All Over Again
(JAMBCO JOV 9 - JANUARY 1993)
Bed Of Roses/Starting All Over Again/Lay Your Hands On Me (live)
(JAMBCO JOV XP 9 - JANUARY 1993)
Bed Of Roses/Starting All Over Again
(JAMBCO JOVMC 9 - JANUARY 1993)
Bed Of Roses/Lay Your Hands On Me (live)/Tokyo Road (live)/I'll Be There For You (live)
(JAMBCO JOV CD 9 - JANUARY 1993)
In These Arms/Bed Of Roses (acoustic)
(JAMBCO JOV 10 LIMITED EDITION ETCHED DISC - MAY 1993)
In These Arms/Blaze Of Glory (live)
(JAMBCO JOV MB 10 LIMITED EDITION BOXED CASSETTE WITH COMMEMORATIVE TOUR PASS - MAY 1993)
In These Arms/Keep The Faith (live)/In These Arms (live)
(JAMBCO JOV CD 10 - MAY 1993)
In These Arms/Bed Of Roses (acoustic)
(JAMBCO JOV MC 10 - MAY 1993)
I'll Sleep When I'm Dead/Never Say Goodbye (live acoustic)
(JAMBCO JOV 11 - JULY 1993)
I'll Sleep When I'm Dead/Never Say Goodbye (live acoustic)
(JAMBCO JOV MC 11 - JULY 1993)
I'll Sleep When I'm Dead/Blaze Of Glory (live)/Wild In The Streets (live)
(JAMBCO JOV CD11 - JULY 1993)
I'll Sleep When I'm Dead/Blaze Of Glory (live)/You Give Love A Bad Name (live)/Bad Medicine (live)
(JAMBCO JOV D11 - JULY 1993)
I Believe (Clearmountain Mix)/I Believe (live)
(JAMBCO JOV 12 - SEPTEMBER 1993)
I Believe (Clearmountain Mix)/I Believe (live)
(JAMBCO JOV MC 12 - SEPTEMBER 1993)
I Believe (Clearmountain Mix)/You Give Love A Bad Name (live)/Born To Be My Baby (live)/Living On A Prayer (live)/Wanted: Dead Or Alive (live)
(JAMBCO JOV CL 12 - SEPTEMBER 1993)
I Believe (Clearmountain Mix)/Runaway (live)/Living On A Prayer (live)/Wanted: Dead Or Alive (live)
(JAMBCO JOV D 12 - SEPTEMBER 1993)
Dry County/Stranger In This Town (live)
(JAMBCO JOV 13 - MARCH 1994)
Dry County/Stranger In This Town (live)
(JAMBCO JOV MC 13 - MARCH 1994)
Dry County/Stranger In This Town (live)/Blood Money (live)
(JAMBCO JOV BX CD 13 - MARCH 1994)
Dry County/It's Only Rock'N'Roll (live)/Waltzing Matilda (live)
(JAMBCO JOV CD 13 - MARCH 1994)
Always (edit)/Always (full length)
(JAMBCO JOV MC 14 - SEPTEMBER 1994)
Always (full length)/Always (edit)/The Boys Are Back In Town
(JAMBCO JOV G 14 - SEPTEMBER 1994)
Always (full length)/Always (edit)/Edge Of A Broken Heart
(JAMBCO JOV CD 14 - SEPTEMBER 1994)
Always (edit)/Always (full length)/Edge Of A Broken Heart/Prayer 94
(JAMBCO JOV CX 14 - SEPTEMBER 1994)
Please Come Home For Christmas/I Wish Everyday Could Be Like Christmas/Back Door Santa
(JAMBCO JOV CD 16 - DECEMBER 1994)
Please Come Home For Christmas/Back Door Santa
(JAMBCO JOV MC 16 - DECEMBER 1994)
Please Come Home For Christmas/Back Door Santa
(JAMBCO JOV P 16 PICTURE DISC - DECEMBER 1994)
Someday I'll Be Saturday Night/Always (live)
(JAMBCO JOV P 15 - FEBRUARY 1995)
Someday I'll Be Saturday Night/Always (live)
(JAMBCO JOV MC 15 - FEBRUARY 1995)
Someday I'll Be Saturday Night/Good Guys Don't Always Wear White/With A Little Help From My Friends (live)/Always (live)
(JAMBCO JOV CX 15 - FEBRUARY 1995)
Someday I'll Be Saturday Night/Good Guys Don't Always Wear White/Always (live)/Someday I'll Be Saturday Night (live)
(JAMBCO JOV DD 15 - FEBRUARY 1995)
These Days/Rocking In The Free World (live)/(It's Hard) Letting You Go
(JAMBCO/MERCURY JOV MC 20 - FEBRUARY 1996)
These Days/Someday I'll Be Saturday Night/These Days (live)/Helter Skelter (live)
(JAMBCO/MERCURY JOV CD 20 - FEBRUARY 1996)

ALBUMS

BON JOVI
Runaway/She Don't Know Me/Love Lies/Breakout/Roulette/Shot Through The Heart/Burning For Love/Come Back/Get Ready.
(VERTIGO VERL 14 – APRIL 1984)

7800 DEGREES FAHRENHEIT
The Price Of Love/In And Out Of Love/Always Run To You/Only Lonely/King Of The Mountain/The Hardest Part Is The Night/To The Fire/Silent Night/Secret Dreams/Tokyo Road.
(VERTIGO VERL 24 – APRIL 1985)

SLIPPERY WHEN WET
Pink Flamingos/Let It Rock/You Give Love A Bad Name/Living On A Prayer/Wanted: Dead Or Alive/Social Disease/Never Say Goodbye/Wild In the Streets/I'd Die For You/Raise Your Hands/Without Love.
(VERTIGO VERH 38 – SEPTEMBER 1986)

NEW JERSEY
Lay Your Hands On Me/Born To Be My Baby/Bad Medicine/Living In Sin/Wild Is The Wind/99 In The Shade/Blood On Blood/Homebound/Ride Cowboy Ride/I'll Be There For You/Stick To Your Guns/Love For Sale.
(VERTIGO VERH 62 – SEPTEMBER 1988)

KEEP THE FAITH
I Believe/Keep The Faith/I'll Sleep When I'm Dead/In These Arms/Bed Of Roses/If I Was Your Mother/Dry Country/Woman In Love/Fear/I Want You/Blame It On The Love Of Rock & Roll/Little Bit Of Soul/Save A Prayer.
(JAMBCO/MERCURY 514 917–2 – OCTOBER 1992)

CROSS ROAD – THE BEST OF BON JOVI
Living On A Prayer/Keep The Faith/ Always/ Wanted: Dead Or Alive/Lay Your Hands On Me/ You Give Love A Bad Name/Bed Of Roses/Blaze Of Glory/In These Arms/Bad Medicine/ I'll Be There For You/In And Out Of Love / Runaway/ Never Say Goodbye
(JAMBCO/MERCURY 522 936–2 – OCTOBER 1994)

THESE DAYS
Hey God/Something For The Pain/This Ain't A Love Song/These Days/Lie To Me/Damned/My Guitar Lies Bleeding In My Arms/(It's Hard) Letting You Go/Hearts Breaking Even/ Something To Believe In/If That's What It Takes/Diamond Ring/All I Want Is Everything/Bitter Wine
(JAMBCO/MERCURY 522 936 - 2 – JUNE 1995)

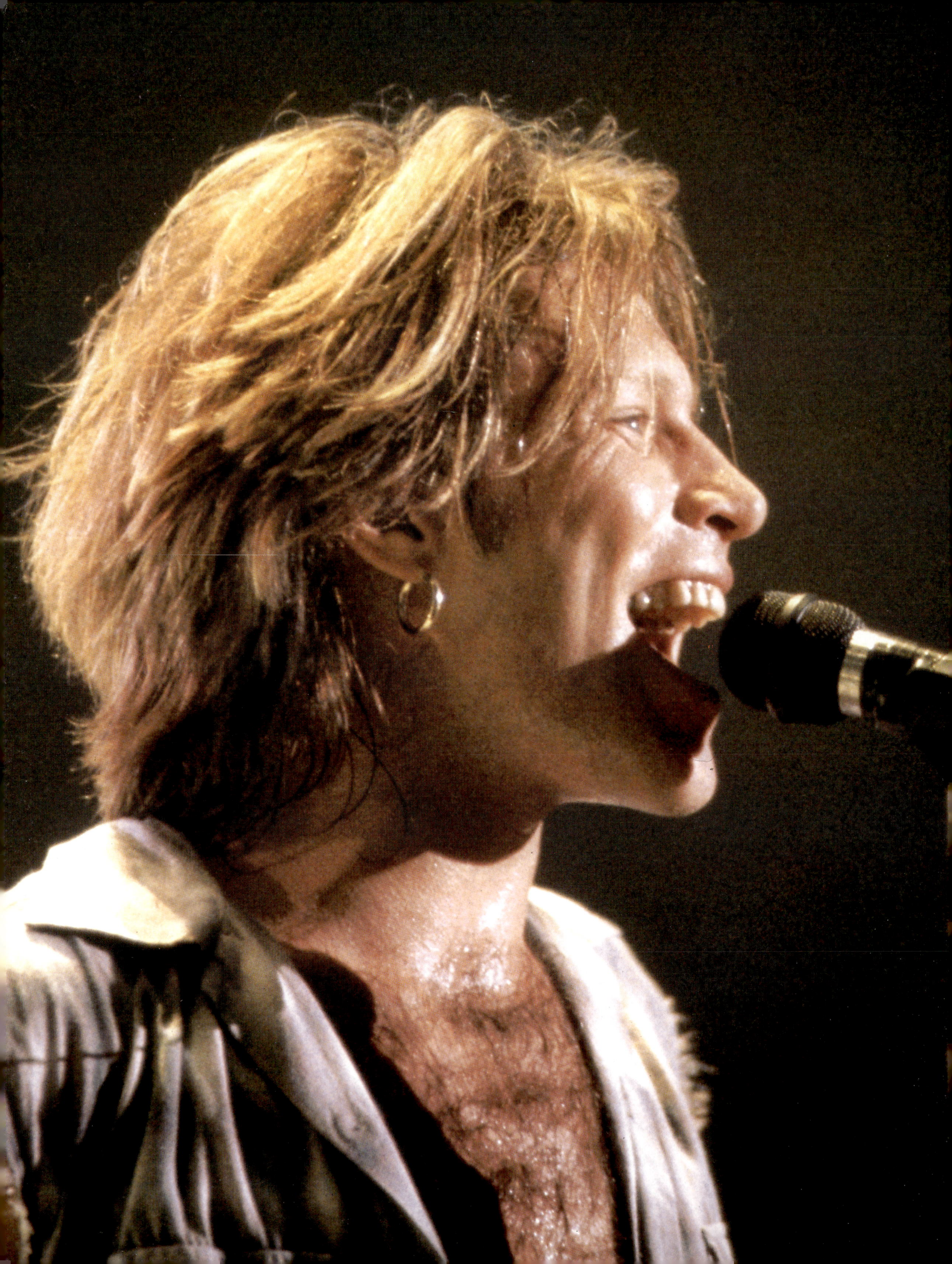

OMNIBUS PRESS

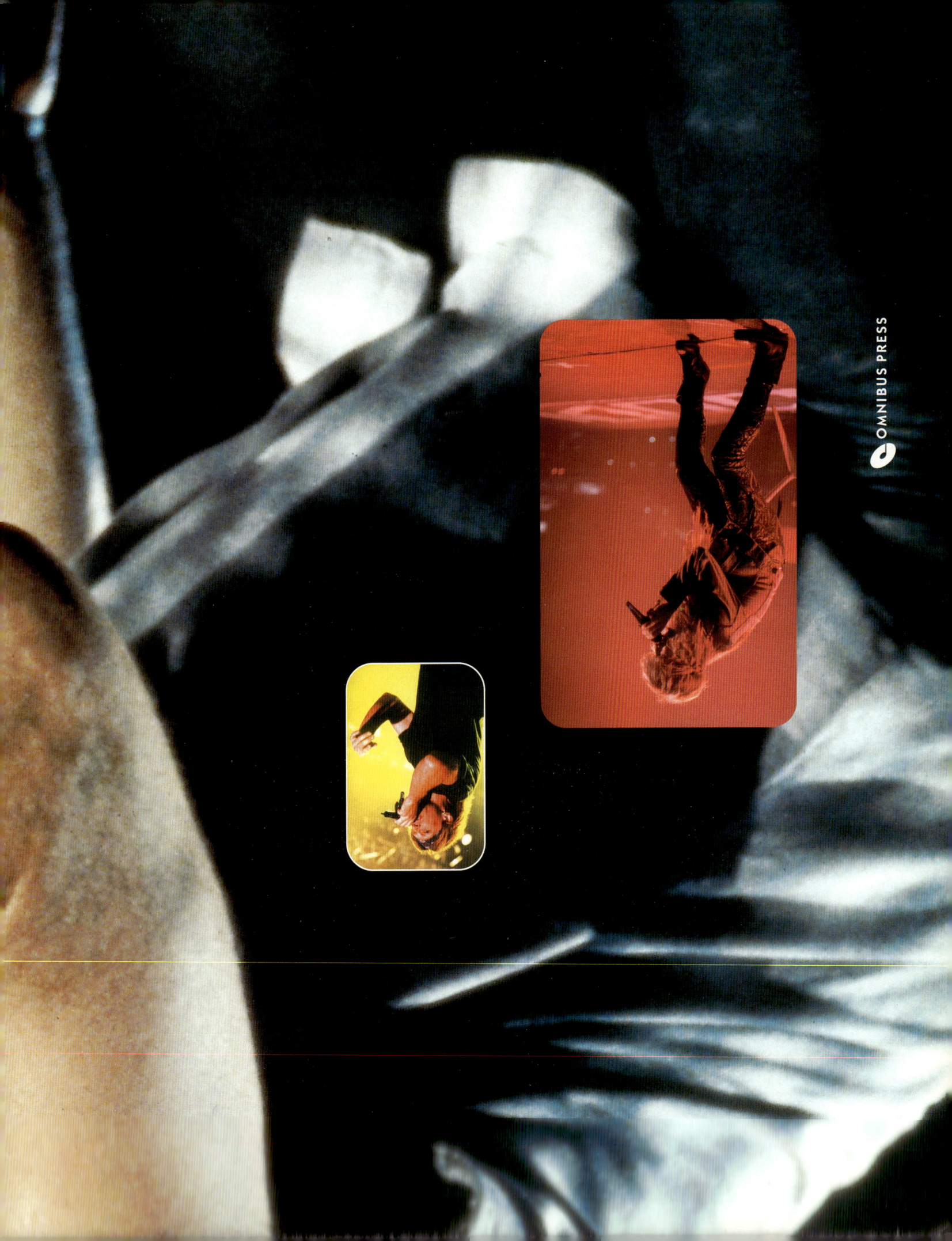

Bon

Jovi
live!